Shame/Guilt Struggles?

Don Barnes

Published by Don Barnes, 2024.

This publication provides the Author's opinion and neither the publisher nor the author intends to render legal, accounting, or other professional advice with this publication.
The publisher and the author disclaim any personal liability, loss or risk incurred as a consequence of the use and application, directly or indirectly, of advice, information or methods presented in this publication.
First Edition

Copyright © 2025

By Don Barnes / Tryune Works!

TRYUNE WORKS! and Life works in threes are trademarks and copyrights of Don Barnes and Tryune Works!

 **LifeWorksInThrees.com**

Table of Contents

About the Author

Don is the founder and author of Life Works in Threes!™ E-books. He is a lifelong Texan who has traveled extensively while taking a keen interest in human behavior. His curiosity about life and what drives humans led him to the discovery of how life works in threes. He coined this term as the *Tryune Concept.*

Don attended college on an athletic scholarship and then embarked on a 30-year career in the oil and gas industry. Since the year 2000, he has been a consultant for distributors and manufacturers of various industries. Along the way, he worked on his Tryune discovery in hopes of someday sharing his findings with those struggling unnecessarily... in life. What Don surmised from 40+ years of R&D was that people were struggling unnecessarily because they were not aware that "life works in threes." They, for the most part, have been living their lives <u>by chance</u> rather than <u>by choice,</u> he also discovered.

From this, he began focusing on the "mechanics of life" which shows formulas for success with subjects such as *life, health, money, purpose and so forth.* When people are able to grasp the Tryune Concept, they can apply the formulas with topics that interest them and begin eliminating the struggle. This epiphany is what triggered his Tryune venture and is now on the path of sharing with all who desire to improve on their lives.

Don currently resides in Southern California and Texas while overseeing his businesses and investments.

Life Works in Threes™

When I was a kid growing up, no one sat me down and said, "Okay Don, I'm going to show you how life works so that you can navigate your way through adulthood." I graduated from school, got married and went about my way with the "learn as you go" concept. It was kind of like putting together a backyard swing set without a set of instructions. Lots of frustration and do-overs, for sure!

My discovery of the "triune" word and noticing how things come together in threes is really what set me off on researching that maybe "life comes in three" ...sort of a mechanical approach to managing life, if you will. I combed the libraries and bookstores for information on this and found one book on the subject that was written back in 1951. The author's name was John S. Arant.

What Mr. Arant had to say is this "For lack of a better name, I have called this *The Triangle of Triumph* and therefore, consistent with the name, since most of these conclusions are built on the geometric figure of the triangle." He continued "All Life and all lives are seated in, and circumscribed by, the triangle. The Author and Source and Director of all life is Himself triune in character – Father, Son, and Holy Spirit. Man is of triple nature – body, mind, and spirit – and within those three there are many triangles – desires, development, decay; intellect, will, sensibilities. Of this "paced interlude in the midst of eternity" which we call time there is the triangle of Past, Present, and Future. Space – that limitless and measureless element of the physical universe – is best known in terms of Height, Breadth, and Depth. Try building yourself some triangles along the lines of your Will, your Work, your Way – You will find some interesting angles.

So, for the first time, I realized that life is designed in a mechanical way to come in threes. That means you don't have to rely on wishing and hoping things turn out okay. You can actually look at the three parts that a particular thing is made of and then apply them to get what you're wanting. Like a three-ingredient recipe or a combination lock. With a combination lock, you need the three exact numbers to unlock the lock...otherwise you will continue to struggle.

Some 40 years later, I accumulated things that work in threes and that's when I knew I needed to share this with anyone wanting answers. To have success/harmony in your life, just apply the three parts of an area you're working on, and things will fall into place. I also learned that the recipe for success with just about anything is by doing these three things, consistently – THINK positively, SPEAK positively and ACT positively. For example, if I want to be a successful artist. I would think to myself "I can do this because I have the talent." Then I would speak it this way "Yes, I am working on my art degree and plan to do portraits professionally." Finally, I would act on that by taking art classes and continue crafting my skill. Eventually, I will see the positive results/success I'm looking for.

Conversely, if I think positively but speak negatively...it will cancel out. Or if I speak positively but have no positive action going on...nothing will happen.

I looked up "How Life Works" and "The Mechanics of Life" and these are really talking about the biology of how our cells work and other chemistry. TRYUNE WORKS! teaches that life is kind of like building blocks. Pick a topic you may be struggling with. See the three parts that topic consists of and then start applying them...on a consistent basis. That will help you overcome the struggle and get you back in harmony/success with how life works.

For 30+ years I was a golf instructor (by accident). My two kids had some success playing junior golf and so friends and neighbors would ask me to show them and their kids how to play golf successfully. From all of this, I got pretty good at watching golfers on the driving range and could spot right away why they were struggling with hitting bad golf shots. I was able to do that because I knew the three steps to hitting good golf shots. I learned them from studying golf and played for several decades. I "broke the code" for me so to speak.

So now you know that life works in threes. You can live your life *by choice* rather than *by chance* and that my friend... is the key to a fulfilling life.

LIFE WORKS
IN THREES!

My sanctuary on the Pacific coast

Introduction

Shame and guilt are powerful emotions that can significantly impact a person's mental and emotional well-being. Shame often stems from a deep-seated feeling of inadequacy or unworthiness, where individuals believe that their entire self is flawed. This pervasive sense of shame can lead to a distorted self-image, where one's value is constantly questioned. Unlike guilt, which is typically associated with specific actions or behaviors, shame affects the core of a person's identity, making it a more insidious and damaging force. This chronic sense of not measuring up can result in social withdrawal, anxiety, and depression, as individuals attempt to hide their perceived flaws from others.

Guilt, on the other hand, arises from recognizing that one has done something wrong or failed to meet one's own moral standards. It often involves a sense of remorse and the desire to make amends. While guilt can be constructive, prompting corrective actions and personal growth, it can also become debilitating if it is excessive or unresolved. Individuals struggling with guilt may ruminate over their mistakes, leading to feelings of helplessness and self-punishment. This internal conflict can hinder their ability to forgive themselves and move forward, trapping them in a cycle of regret and self-reproach.

Together, shame and guilt can create a complex emotional landscape where individuals feel trapped by their own perceived failings. The struggle with these emotions often involves a delicate balance between acknowledging one's mistakes and maintaining a sense of self-worth. Supportive relationships and therapeutic interventions can play crucial roles in helping individuals navigate these feelings, promoting self-compassion and healthier coping strategies. Understanding and addressing the roots of shame and guilt can lead to personal growth and a more positive self-view, fostering resilience and emotional well-being.

My discovery of the Tryune Concept

Before we dive into shame/guilt struggles and how to overcome them, let me share my discovery of the Tryune Concept and how life works in threes. It all began in the summer of 1982.

I grew up with parents who treated everyone with decency and respect. My three older sisters and I were raised in a home that was "middle-class traditional." We lived in modest homes in different small towns, attended school and church on a regular basis and celebrated all the traditional holidays. Eventually we settled during the spring of 1964 in the big city of Houston, Texas. I'll never forget the vastness of the city and hearing sirens from police cars, fire trucks and ambulances on a regular basis. I was excited and scared at the same time.

Once settled in this fast-paced city, I finished my growing-up years with an academic diploma and sweetheart intact. I got a job, bought a car, got married, bought a house and produced two beautiful babies in a span of about 5 years. Talk about having to grow up fast!

Things went from great in my childhood to absolute misery in my young adulthood. I began to struggle with my job because deep down I just hated what I was doing. This problem created a snowball effect because soon after, my weight, my finances, my relationships, my happiness and everything else worth saving was going down the drain. I eventually hit a level of frustration that I had never experienced before and didn't know how to get out of it. My cry for help was for anyone or anything to come to my rescue. I just ran out of solutions for my situation.

This is when my discovery happened.

One night shortly after my meltdown, while sleeping soundly, the word "triune" began to softly pound in my head like a mantra. I woke up a little startled and decided to go look up the word in my favorite dictionary (this was WAY before Google.) The definition said '**triune** (try-une) – 1) a group of three things; united. 2) Being 3 in 1 such as *humans are mental, physical and spiritual.* I scratched my head, got a glass of water and went back to bed.

The next day while driving around town, I began thinking about things that I was taught in my younger years that came in threes. My Boy Scout manual taught that to have **character**, I needed to be *1) physically strong, 2) mentally awake and 3) morally straight.* My high school football coach would say emphatically "If you want to be **a good football player**, you have to be *1) mobile 2) agile and 3) hostile!*" My first sales manager shared with me that to be **a successful salesman**, I needed to have *1) sales skills, 2) product knowledge and 3) a good image.*

"Hmm", I thought, "wonder if there are other examples out there of things that work in threes?" So, some 40 years later, I have researched and discovered that many, many things work in threes. What this message was telling me is that to achieve success or balance in any significant area of my life, the three things that area consisted of had to be present continuously. That's when I had my epiphany. This discovery was telling me the secret to how life <u>really</u> works.

Tryune is a play on the word "triune" as an invitation to "try" this concept. Furthermore, we do not say that life <u>only</u> works in threes. Life also works in ones, twos, fours and so on. What has been observed though is that the many things significant to life, just so happen to come and work in threes. That's what is being shared in this book.

Now, you are about to see 40+ years of research and proof that life works in threes. I did not make up any of these topics. I invite you to research them on the internet to validate what is written here. There are some interesting facts that most of us have never realized...until now.

How Life Works in Threes (around 200 examples)

<u>LIFE</u>

Humans consist of *body, mind and soul.*

A human's basic needs are *health, income and provisions.*

A human's basic wants are *comfort, gain and approval.*

Our minds are made up of the *conscious, the subconscious and the unconscious.*

Philosophy explains *the id, the ego and superego.*

Atoms consist of *protons, neutrons and electrons.*

Motion is explained by *three basic laws.*

Science falls under three main branches: *natural, social and formal sciences*

Time is *past, present and future*...at the same time.

Electricity consists of *ohms, amperes and voltage.*

Music's basic elements are *duration, pitch and timbre.*

Democracy is a government *of the people, by the people and for the people.*

U.S. branches of government are *the judicial, the executive and the legislative.*

Armed Forces protect us on *land, air and sea.*

Environmentally, we are asked *to reduce, recycle and re-use.*

The news program gives us *the news, sports and conditions.*

Our days consist of *morning, afternoon and evening.*

Three months in each season of the year

Our main meals are known as *breakfast, lunch and dinner.*

A balanced diet consists of *good proteins, carbohydrates and fats.*

Traditional Family consists of *father, mother, and child(ren)*

SCIENCES

Three major branches of natural science – *(physical, earth/space and life sciences)*

Three major branches of modern physics - *(classical, relativistic, quantum)*

Three major branches of biology *(botany, zoology, microbiology)*

Three spatial dimensions: *height* (up/down), *width* (left/right) and *depth* (forwards/backwards)

Three-gauge bosons (photon, gluon, W&Z bosons)

Three types of elementary particles *(leptons, quarks, gauge bosons)*

Three quarks in every proton *(two "up" and one "down")*

Three primary colors of light *(red, green, blue)*

Three color tone properties *(hue, value, chroma)*

Three laws of motion (*Newton's laws*)

Three laws of planetary motion (*Kepler's laws*)

Three layers of the Sun's interior (*core, radiative zone, convective zone*)

Three layers of the Sun's atmosphere (*photosphere, chromosphere, corona*)

Three types of meteorites (*iron, stony iron, stony*)

Three types of galaxy shapes (*elliptical, spiral, irregular*)

Three substances of the universe (*normal matter, 'dark matter', 'dark energy'*)

Three phases of the moon (*new moon, first quarter, full moon*)

Three planetary regions (*temperate, sub-tropical, tropical*)

Three layers of the Earth (*crust, mantle, core*)

Three components of an ecosystem (*producers, consumers, decomposers*)

Three types of rocks (*igneous, sedimentary, metamorphic*)

Three types of fossil fuels (*coal, crude oil, natural gas*)

Three hydrological processes (*evaporation, condensation, precipitation*)

Three basic types of (meteorological) precipitation (*liquid, freezing, frozen*)

Three types of substances (*mono-constituent, multi-constituent, UVCB*)

Three phases of (normal) matter (*solid, liquid, gas*)

Three types of covalent chemical bonds (*single, double and triple bonds*)

Three isotopes of hydrogen (*protium, deuterium, tritium*)

Three atoms in each molecule of water (*two hydrogen atoms and an oxygen atom*)

Three endings to salts (*-ide, -ite, -ate*)

Three requirements for fire (*fuel, oxygen, heat*)

Three nucleotide bases in a genetic codon

Three domains of life (*archaea, bacteria and eukaryotes*)

Three major groups of flowering plants (*monocots, eudicots, magnolids*)

Three major functions that are basic to plant growth and development: (*photosynthesis* [making sugars], *respiration* [metabolizing those sugars], and *transpiration* [water vapor loss]

Three things that the chlorophyll in plants needs for photosynthesis to take place: (*sunlight, carbon dioxide and water*)

Transpiration serves three roles: (*cooling the plant, moving minerals* and *sugars through the plant*, and *maintaining the turgidity pressure* [stiffness] *of the plant's cells*)

Three parts of an insect's body (*head, thorax, abdomen*)

BIOLOGY

Three types of cones in the retina, relating to the three primary colors

Three semi-circular canals in the ear (*lateral, anterior, posterior*)

Three sections in the ear (*outer, middle, inner*)

Three ossicles in the middle ear (*malleus, incus, stapes*)

Three segments to each limb (*proximal, mid, distal*)

Three bones in each arm (*humerus, radius, ulna*)

Three joints in the arm (*shoulder, elbow, wrist*)

Three joints in the leg (*hip, knee, ankle*)

Three joints in the elbow (*humeroulnar, humeroradial, proximal radioulnar*)

Three functional compartments in the knee joint (*the femoropatellar, medial femorotibial* and *lateral femorotibial articulations*)

Three types of fibrous joints (*sutures, gomphoses, syndesmoses*)

Three types of bone in each hand (*carpals, metacarpals, phalanges*)

Three types of bone in each foot (*tarsals, metatarsals, phalanges*)

Three bones (phalanges) in each finger and in each toe (*proximal, intermediate, distal*)

Three layers of skin (*dermis, epidermis, hypodermis*)

Three components of a cell (*cell membrane, nucleus, cytoplasm*)

Three types of blood vessels (*arteries, veins, capillaries*)

Three types of blood cells [*red* (erythrocytes), *white* (leukocytes), *platelets* (thrombocytes)]

Three processes of the intestinal tract (*ingestion, digestion, excretion*)

Three germ layers (*Endoderm, Mesoderm, Ectoderm*)

Three parts of a human tooth (*crown, neck, root*)

Three organs of otolaryngology (*ear, nose, throat*)

Three major body systems (*digestive, circulatory, respiratory*)

Three parts to a neuron: (*soma* [*cell body*], *axon, dendrites*)

Three main parts of the brain (*forebrain, midbrain, hindbrain*)

Three parts of the forebrain (*cerebrum, thalamus, hypothalamus*)

Three parts of the midbrain (*colliculi, tegmentum, cerebral peduncles*)

Three parts of the hindbrain (*cerebellum, pons, medulla*)

Three membranes enclosing the brain (*dura mater, arachnoid, pia mater*)

The brain operates on three levels: *consciously* (for cognitive thought and declarative memory); *subconsciously* (for pre-planned actions and procedural memory); and *unconsciously* (for breathing, heart beating, etc.)

Our conscious mind is fed from three sources: *our senses* (which can be fooled); *our memory* (which is flawed); and *our imagination* (which is inventive)

Three aspects of the human mind (*memory, intellect, will*)

Three parts of the human personality (*id, ego, superego*)

The sum of human capacity consists of three abilities (*thought, word and deed*)

Three times of man (*birth, life, death*)

Three periods of the Gait Cycle (*initial double limb support, single limb support, and terminal double limb support*)

MUSIC

Three types of musical notes (*sharps, flats, naturals*)

Three aspects of a song (*lyrics, melody, rhythm*)

Three types of musical chords (*root, third, fifth*)

MATHEMATICS

Three types of a real number (*positive, negative, zero*)

Three parts to any arithmetic operation: for addition: *augend, addend and sum* - for subtraction: *minuend, subtrahend and difference* - for multiplication: *multiplicand, multiplier and product* - for division: *dividend, divisor and quotient*

Three laws of arithmetic operations (*commutative, associative, distributive*)

Three types of equivalence relation (*reflexivity, symmetry, transitivity*)

Three types of symmetry operations (*translation, rotation, reflection*)

Three geometries (*Euclidean, spherical, hyperbolic*)

The number *3* is the basis of an entire branch of mathematics, called trigonometry (from the Greek *trigonon* "triangle" + *metron* "measure")

Three trigonometric functions (*sine, cosine, tangent*)

Three types of average (*mean, mode, median*)

<u>GRAMMAR</u>

Three logical operators (*AND, OR and NOT*)

Three laws of logic (*identity, noncontradiction, excluded middle*)

Three parts of a logical syllogism (*major premise, minor premise, conclusion*)

Three grammatical parts to a sentence (*subject, verb, complement*)

Three persons in grammar [*1st person* (I/we), *2nd* (you or your), *3rd* (he/she/it/they)]

Three genders in grammar [*masculine* (he/him), *feminine* (she/her), *neuter* (it)]

Three forms of comparison in grammar [*positive, comparative* (more, -er), *superlative* (most, -est)]

Three cases in (English) grammar [*subjective/nominative* (he), *objective/accusative* (him) and *possessive/genitive* (his)]

Three parts of a narrative (*beginning, middle, end*)

Components of an essay (*introduction, body, conclusion*)

Elements of a rhetorical appeal (*ethos, pathos, logos*)

Aspects of a story (*plot, characters, setting*)

<u>RELIGION</u>

The Creator – *omniscient, omnipotent, omnipresent*

Christian God – *Father, Son, Holy Spirit*

Jesus – *The Way, The Truth, The Life*

Ancient Near East- *Qudshu, Astarte, Anat*

Classical Antiquity – Many dieties came in threes

Hinduism – Para Brahman is *Brahma, Visnu, Shiva*

Ancient Celtic Cultures – *many example of triad dieties*

Buddhism – *The three jewels*

Taoism – *The three pure ones*

Islam – *Fear, Hope and Love*

Baha'i - *Intention, Power and Action*

Confucianism – *Benevolence, Wisdom and Courage*

<u>OTHER TRIUNE EXAMPLES</u>

3 Coins in a Fountain

3 Days of the Condor

3 Miles in a League

3 Goals in a Hat Trick

3 Piece Suit

3 Feet in a Yard

3 Books in Lord of the Rings

3 Ring Circus

3 Ships of Christopher Columbus

3 Sheets to the Wind

3 Books in a Trilogy

3 Wheels on a Tricycle

3 Wise Men

3-Legged Race

3 Ring Circus

3-Wheeler

3 Cornered Hat

3 Dimensional

3 Musketeers

3 R's (reading, 'riting, 'rithmatic)

3 Sides of a triangle

3 Races in the Triple Crown (horse racing)

3 Angles in a Triangle

3 Trimesters in a Pregnancy

3 Flavors in Neapolitan Ice Cream

3 Stars in Orion's belt

3 Barleycorns in an Inch

3 Hands on a Clock (with the Seconds Hand)

3 Colors in a Flag

3 Minute Egg

3 Great Pyramids at Giza

3 Holes in a Bowling Ball

3 Colors in a Set of Traffic Lights

3 Minutes in a Boxing Round

3 Teaspoons in a Tablespoon

3 Legs on a Stool

3 Monastic Vows (Obience, Stability, Conversatio Morum)

3 Body Types: Endomorph, Mesomorph, Ectomorph

3 Ring Notebooks

3 Germ layers: Endoderm, Mesoderm, Ectoderm

3 Species of Homo: Homo habilis, Homo erectus, Homo sapiens

3 Basic parts of a camera: Lens, Shutter, Sensor

3 Stages of a Project lifecycle: initiation, planning, execution

The Truth, The Whole Truth and Nothing but the Truth

Life, Liberty and the Pursuit of Happiness

Hear no Evil, See no Evil, Speak no Evil

National motto of France/Haiti: Liberty, Equality, Fraternity

Paper, Rock, Scissors

Ready, Aim, Fire

On Your mark, Get Set, Go

Olympic medals of gold, silver, bronze

Types of joints (ball & socket, hinge, pivot)

Stages of a rocket launch (launch, orbit, re-entry)

Parts of a joke (setup, delivery, punchline)

Primary components of a transistor (emitter, base, collector)

Primary components of an airplane (fuselage, wings, empennage)

Basic components of a computer: CPU, memory, storage

Three phases in the development of technology (*eotechnic* [*mechanical*], *paleotechnic* [*steam-powered*] and *neotechnic* [*electric-powered*]

Communication systems require three components (*transmitter, channel, receiver*)

The list goes on. See if you can find more examples as they are everywhere in our universe! Now that you know that life works in threes (with proof!), we can begin to apply this concept to whatever topics we want.

So, to overcome struggles with shame/guilt, we need to apply the three areas that shame/guilt consists of – DIFFERENCES, DANGER and RECOVERY. Let's get started!

DIFFERENCES
SHAME/GUILT
DANGER
RECOVERY

SHAME/GUILT

While related, shame and guilt are distinct emotions that affect individuals in different ways. Shame is a deep, often overwhelming feeling that one's entire self is flawed or inadequate. It is rooted in the belief that there is something fundamentally wrong with the person, not just their actions. This pervasive sense of worthlessness can lead to severe self-criticism, social isolation, and mental health issues like depression and anxiety. Because shame attacks the core of a person's identity, it often results in a defensive response where individuals may withdraw, hide their true selves, or engage in destructive behaviors to avoid facing their perceived shortcomings. The **danger** of shame lies in its ability to erode self-esteem and foster a pervasive sense of hopelessness.

Guilt, in contrast, focuses on specific actions or behaviors rather than the self as a whole. It arises from the recognition that one has done something wrong or failed to meet one's own moral or ethical standards. Guilt can serve as a catalyst for positive change by motivating individuals to make amends and improve their behavior. However, excessive guilt or guilt that is not properly addressed can become harmful. It may lead to chronic self-reproach, anxiety, and difficulties in self-forgiveness. If not managed constructively, guilt can become a source of ongoing distress, as individuals may continuously berate themselves for past mistakes.

Recovery from both shame and guilt involves different approaches but shares some common elements. For shame, effective recovery often requires fostering self-compassion and rebuilding a positive self-image. Therapeutic techniques such as cognitive-behavioral therapy can help individuals challenge and reframe their negative beliefs about themselves, promoting a healthier self-concept. Building supportive relationships and engaging in activities that affirm one's worth can also aid in overcoming shame. For guilt, recovery involves acknowledging mistakes, making amends where possible, and practicing self-forgiveness. Developing a growth mindset, where mistakes are viewed as opportunities for learning rather than indications of personal failure, can help mitigate excessive guilt. Both emotions benefit from a supportive network, professional guidance, and the cultivation of self-acceptance and understanding.

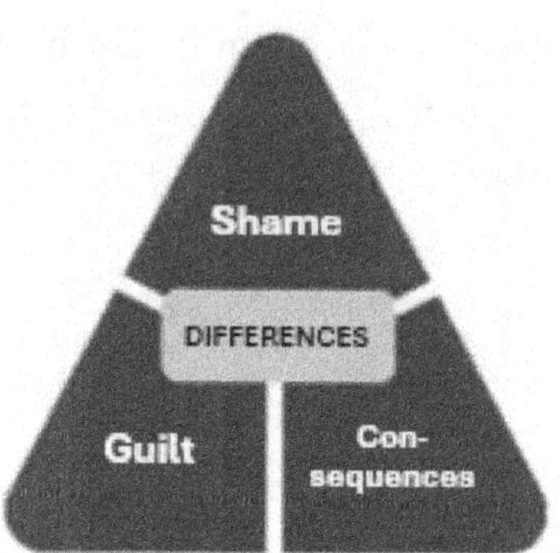

Shame
DIFFERENCES
Guilt
Con-
sequences

DIFFERENCES

From a psychological perspective, **shame** and **guilt** are distinct in their core dynamics and effects on the individual's self-concept. **Shame** is a self-focused emotion that relates to one's identity and sense of worth. It emerges when an individual feels that they are fundamentally flawed or inadequate. This internalized sense of unworthiness can deeply impact one's self-esteem and lead to feelings of powerlessness. Psychologically, shame often manifests as a global, negative evaluation of the self, where the person believes their entire being is defective, rather than focusing on a specific behavior. This pervasive self-criticism can result in chronic emotional distress, avoidance behaviors, and a strong fear of exposure or rejection.

Guilt, on the other hand, is behavior-focused and relates to the acknowledgment of a specific wrongdoing or failure to meet personal standards. It involves a recognition that one's actions have negatively affected others or failed to align with one's own moral values. From a psychological standpoint, guilt is often associated with a desire to rectify the situation and make amends. This emotion typically prompts a more targeted response, such as apologizing, making reparations, or changing future behavior. Unlike shame, which can lead to withdrawal and self-criticism, guilt often motivates constructive actions and problem-solving, facilitating personal growth and moral development.

The **psychological consequences of shame and guilt** diverge significantly due to their different focuses. **Shame** can be more destructive as it undermines the individual's entire self-concept, potentially leading to severe emotional problems such as depression, anxiety, and social withdrawal. It often results in a defensive posture where individuals may avoid confronting their flaws or may become isolated. In contrast, **guilt** tends to be more adaptive, as it encourages individuals to recognize their mistakes and seek corrective actions. However, excessive guilt or unresolved guilt can still be problematic, potentially leading to ongoing self-reproach and stress. Effective management of both emotions often requires therapeutic interventions to address their root causes and promote healthier self-perceptions and behaviors.

Shame
DIFFERENCES
Guilt
Con-
sequences

Shame

The origin of **shame** is deeply rooted in both evolutionary and social contexts. Psychologically, shame can be traced back to early human societies where social cohesion and group acceptance were crucial for survival. Early humans relied on social bonds for protection, resources, and communal living, making the approval of others essential. Shame likely evolved as a mechanism to enforce social norms and discourage behaviors that could jeopardize group harmony. When individuals violated these norms or failed to meet social expectations, feelings of shame would arise, prompting corrective behavior and promoting adherence to group standards. This evolutionary perspective suggests that shame helped maintain social order and cohesion by regulating individual behavior through internalized social pressures.

In contemporary society, **shame** is often addressed through various social mechanisms and cultural practices. Social institutions such as families, schools, and religious organizations play significant roles in shaping and reinforcing social norms, which in turn influence the experience of shame. For instance, educational systems and parenting practices often emphasize the importance of conformity and adherence to societal expectations, sometimes using shame as a tool for behavior correction. Public shaming has also been a historical practice, where individuals were ostracized or humiliated to enforce moral standards and deter misconduct. While this method may have been effective in promoting compliance, it often exacerbates feelings of shame and can lead to further social alienation.

In modern times, there is a growing recognition of the negative impacts of shame and a shift towards more supportive approaches. Contemporary psychological and therapeutic practices emphasize addressing shame with empathy and self-compassion rather than through punitive measures. Mental health professionals often focus on helping individuals understand the roots of their shame and develop healthier self-perceptions. Societal movements towards inclusivity and understanding aim to reduce the stigmatization of personal struggles and promote environments where individuals feel valued regardless of their perceived shortcomings. This shift reflects a broader understanding of the detrimental effects of shame on mental health and a commitment to fostering a more supportive and compassionate society.

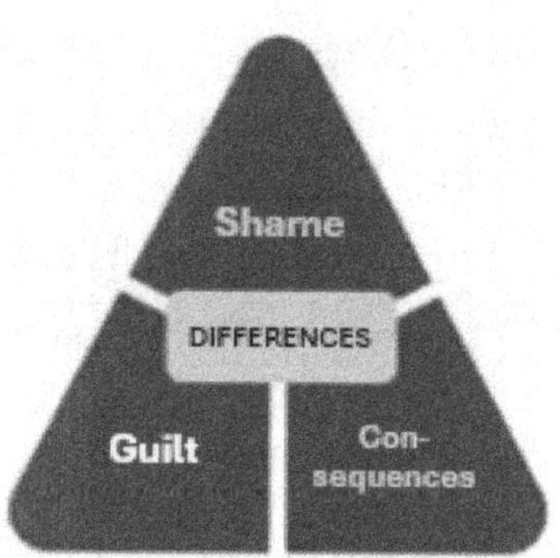
Shame
DIFFERENCES
Guilt
Con-
sequences

Guilt

The origin of **guilt** is deeply intertwined with the development of moral and ethical frameworks within human societies. Evolutionarily, guilt likely emerged as a social mechanism to enforce cooperative behavior and moral standards within groups. Unlike shame, which focuses on the self, guilt is related to specific actions and their consequences. Early human communities required adherence to social norms for mutual survival and success. Guilt would arise when individuals recognized that their actions had violated group norms or caused harm to others, thereby motivating them to rectify their behavior and seek forgiveness. This self-regulation mechanism helped maintain social harmony and trust, essential for the cohesion of early human groups.

In contemporary society, **guilt** is addressed through a combination of cultural, legal, and social practices. Various social institutions, including families, schools, and religious organizations, play a significant role in shaping individuals' moral values and standards. These institutions often use guilt to encourage ethical behavior and accountability. For example, educational systems might use guilt to motivate students to meet academic expectations, while religious teachings often incorporate guilt to foster moral conduct and repentance. Additionally, legal systems may impose guilt through judicial processes, where individuals are held accountable for their actions and required to make amends or face consequences.

Modern approaches to dealing with guilt reflect a nuanced understanding of its role and effects on mental health. Therapeutic practices emphasize the importance of addressing guilt constructively rather than allowing it to become a source of chronic self-reproach. Psychologists and counselors often work with individuals to explore the origins of their guilt, encourage self-forgiveness, and develop strategies for making amends. Societal attitudes towards guilt have also evolved, with increasing recognition of the need for compassion and restorative justice rather than purely punitive measures. This shift highlights a growing commitment to addressing guilt in ways that promote personal growth, accountability, and healing, rather than perpetuating feelings of shame and self-punishment.

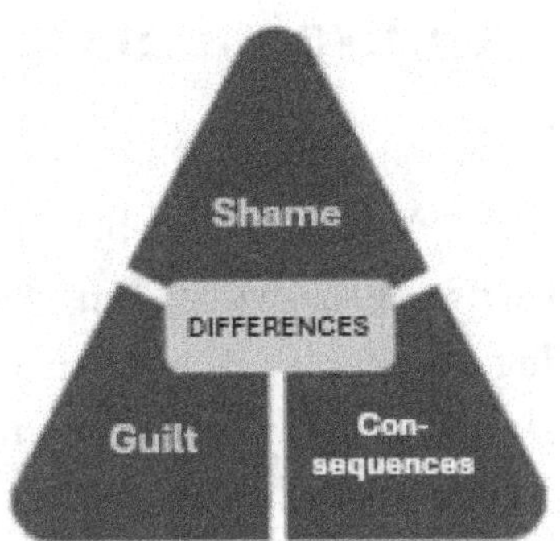
Shame
DIFFERENCES
Guilt
Con-
sequences

Consequences

Allowing **shame** to overtake one's life can have profound and debilitating consequences. When shame becomes pervasive, it often leads to a diminished sense of self-worth and identity. Individuals may internalize their feelings of inadequacy to such an extent that they perceive themselves as fundamentally flawed or unlovable. This can result in chronic emotional distress, including anxiety and depression. The pervasive nature of shame can also lead to social withdrawal, as individuals may avoid social interactions or hide aspects of themselves to prevent further exposure and judgment. Over time, this isolation can exacerbate feelings of loneliness and further erode self-esteem, creating a vicious cycle of self-loathing and disconnection.

Excessive **guilt** can similarly have severe psychological consequences, especially when it becomes pervasive and unresolved. While guilt can initially serve as a motivating force for corrective actions, persistent guilt can lead to chronic self-reproach and emotional strain. Individuals may find themselves caught in a cycle of rumination, where they continually revisit their mistakes without making constructive progress. This constant self-criticism can contribute to stress, anxiety, and depression. Moreover, unresolved guilt can impair one's ability to engage in healthy relationships, as individuals may struggle with feelings of unworthiness or fear of judgment, leading to difficulties in forging and maintaining connections with others.

The consequences of allowing both shame and guilt to dominate one's life extend beyond individual well-being, affecting overall quality of life and interpersonal relationships. When individuals are overwhelmed by these emotions, their capacity for self-compassion and resilience diminishes, making it harder to cope with life's challenges effectively. This can impact their ability to pursue goals, experience joy, and engage meaningfully with others. Addressing these emotions through therapeutic support, self-compassion practices, and social support is crucial for restoring a balanced self-perception and fostering healthier emotional functioning. By confronting and managing shame and guilt constructively, individuals can improve their mental health and enhance their overall life satisfaction.

Toxic
Shame
DANGER
Toxic
Guilt
Non-
Treatment

DANGER

Allowing mental challenges like **shame** and **guilt** to fester within a person can have serious psychological consequences. When these emotions are left unaddressed, they often intensify over time, leading to a deterioration of mental health. Shame can cause individuals to internalize a sense of unworthiness and self-loathing, which may result in chronic anxiety, depression, and a pervasive sense of hopelessness. This internalized negativity can erode self-esteem, making individuals more vulnerable to further emotional distress and mental health disorders. As shame festers, it often becomes more entrenched, creating a barrier to personal growth and emotional healing.

Similarly, **guilt** that is not processed constructively can lead to severe emotional and behavioral repercussions. Persistent guilt can contribute to ongoing self-criticism and rumination, which may exacerbate stress and anxiety. The inability to forgive oneself for perceived wrongdoings can lead to a sense of perpetual remorse, affecting one's overall well-being and daily functioning. In extreme cases, unresolved guilt can cause individuals to engage in self-punitive behaviors, including substance abuse or self-harm, as a way to cope with or escape from their overwhelming feelings of culpability. This cycle of guilt can hinder personal development and lead to further emotional difficulties.

The dangers of letting shame and guilt fester also extend to interpersonal relationships. Individuals who are consumed by these emotions may struggle with intimacy and connection, as their self-perception and fear of judgment can inhibit open and healthy communication. This can result in social withdrawal, strained relationships, and difficulties in forming supportive networks. Moreover, the internal struggles with shame and guilt can affect one's ability to empathize and engage effectively with others, leading to isolation and a reduced quality of life. Addressing these emotions through professional support and self-care is essential for breaking the cycle of suffering and fostering healthier relationships and emotional well-being.

Toxic
Shame
DANGER
Toxic
Guilt
Non-
Treatment

Toxic Shame

Toxic shame carries profound and far-reaching implications for an individual's mental health and overall quality of life. Unlike ordinary shame, which might be fleeting and tied to specific behaviors, toxic shame is a pervasive, deep-seated emotion that affects one's entire self-concept. It leads individuals to view themselves as fundamentally flawed or unworthy. This pervasive sense of unworthiness can manifest as chronic anxiety, depression, and a profound lack of self-esteem. People plagued by toxic shame often struggle with persistent self-criticism and a distorted self-image, which can significantly impair their emotional resilience and ability to cope with life's challenges.

The impact of toxic shame extends beyond individual mental health and can deeply affect personal relationships. Individuals grappling with toxic shame may experience difficulties in forming and maintaining healthy relationships due to their pervasive sense of unworthiness and fear of rejection. This can lead to social withdrawal and isolation, as they may avoid intimate connections to protect themselves from perceived judgment or further humiliation. In relationships, toxic shame can result in dysfunctional patterns of interaction, including excessive self-blame, defensiveness, or difficulty in accepting and giving support. These patterns can create a barrier to genuine emotional intimacy and mutual trust, further exacerbating feelings of isolation and alienation.

The long-term implications of toxic shame also influence one's overall life trajectory and personal growth. The internalized belief of being fundamentally flawed can stifle personal development and inhibit the pursuit of goals and aspirations. Individuals may struggle with motivation and self-efficacy, feeling undeserving of success or fearful of failure. This can prevent them from engaging in opportunities for growth or taking risks that could lead to positive change. Addressing toxic shame through therapeutic interventions, such as cognitive-behavioral therapy or compassion-focused therapy, is crucial for helping individuals reframe their self-perception, build self-esteem, and develop healthier, more fulfilling relationships and life paths.

Toxic
Shame
DANGER
Toxic
Guilt
Non-
Treatment

Toxic Guilt

Toxic guilt can have severe and debilitating implications for an individual's mental and emotional well-being. Unlike constructive guilt, which can prompt corrective actions and personal growth, toxic guilt becomes overwhelming and persistent, leading to chronic self-reproach and emotional suffering. Individuals grappling with toxic guilt often feel an intense, lingering sense of responsibility for their perceived mistakes or shortcomings, which can result in excessive rumination and self-blame. This perpetual guilt can lead to heightened levels of stress, anxiety, and depression, as individuals struggle to escape the weight of their remorse and find relief from their self-imposed punishment.

The effects of toxic guilt extend into personal relationships, where its impact can be equally damaging. Individuals who experience toxic guilt may exhibit patterns of behavior such as excessive apologizing, overcompensating, or withdrawing from others to avoid further perceived wrongdoing. These behaviors can create strain in relationships, as loved ones may find it difficult to engage with someone who is constantly preoccupied with guilt or who may avoid intimacy out of fear of further guilt-inducing actions. This can lead to misunderstandings, conflict, and a breakdown in communication, ultimately eroding trust and emotional connection in relationships.

Furthermore, toxic guilt can impede personal and professional growth by stifling motivation and self-confidence. When individuals are consumed by overwhelming guilt, they may become paralyzed by their fears of making mistakes or failing, leading to avoidance of new opportunities or challenges. This fear of failure and self-criticism can prevent them from pursuing personal goals or achieving their full potential. To mitigate the effects of toxic guilt, it is essential for individuals to engage in therapeutic practices that focus on self-forgiveness, cognitive restructuring, and developing healthier coping mechanisms. By addressing the root causes of toxic guilt and working towards self-compassion, individuals can break free from the cycle of self-punishment and move towards a more balanced and fulfilling life.

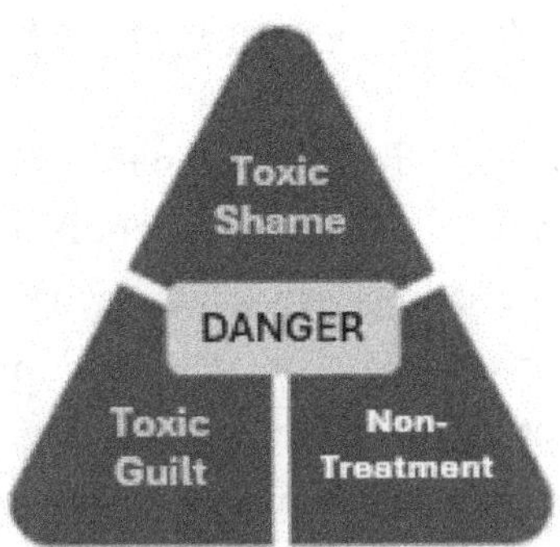
Toxic
Shame
DANGER
Toxic
Guilt
Non-
Treatment

Non-Treatment

Failing to address **shame** and **guilt** complexes can have profound and detrimental effects on an individual's mental and emotional health. When these complex emotions are left untreated, they often become entrenched, leading to persistent feelings of unworthiness and self-blame. This can result in chronic psychological distress, including anxiety and depression. Individuals may experience diminished self-esteem, pervasive self-criticism, and a pervasive sense of hopelessness. The lack of intervention can exacerbate these feelings, making it increasingly difficult to break free from the negative thought patterns and emotional turmoil associated with shame and guilt.

Moreover, untreated shame and guilt complexes can significantly impact personal and professional relationships. Individuals may struggle with intimacy and trust due to their pervasive sense of inadequacy or fear of judgment. This can lead to social withdrawal, avoidance behaviors, and difficulties in forming and maintaining meaningful connections with others. In professional settings, the emotional burden of untreated shame and guilt can hinder one's ability to perform effectively, contribute to chronic stress, and limit career advancement. These interpersonal and professional challenges can further isolate individuals and reinforce their negative self-perception.

In addition, unresolved shame and guilt can impede personal growth and hinder the pursuit of goals. Individuals may become paralyzed by their internal struggles, avoiding new opportunities or challenges out of fear of failure or making further mistakes. This fear-driven paralysis can prevent them from achieving their potential and experiencing personal fulfillment. Addressing these complex emotions through therapeutic interventions, self-compassion practices, and support networks is crucial for fostering emotional resilience, improving self-esteem, and facilitating personal and professional growth. Without such intervention, individuals may remain trapped in a cycle of self-reproach and missed opportunities, limiting their overall quality of life.

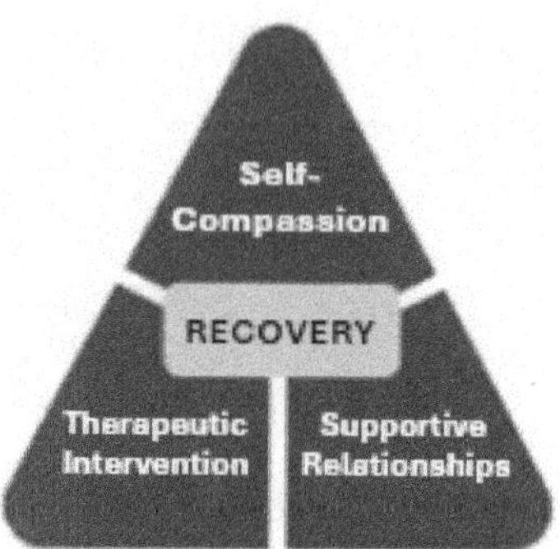

Self-
Compassion
RECOVERY
Therapeutic
Intervention
Supportive
Relationships

RECOVERY

Self-compassion is one of the most critical keys to recovery from shame and guilt issues. Developing self-compassion involves treating oneself with the same kindness and understanding that one would offer to a close friend facing similar struggles. This practice encourages individuals to recognize their own humanity and imperfections without harsh judgment. By cultivating a compassionate inner dialogue, individuals can mitigate the harsh self-criticism associated with shame and guilt. This approach helps to reframe negative self-beliefs, allowing individuals to approach their mistakes and flaws with understanding rather than condemnation. Through self-compassion, individuals can build a healthier self-image and foster emotional resilience, which is essential for healing from deep-seated shame and guilt.

Therapeutic intervention plays a crucial role in addressing and resolving issues related to shame and guilt. Professional therapy, such as cognitive-behavioral therapy (CBT) or compassion-focused therapy, provides a structured approach to understanding and managing these complex emotions. Therapists can help individuals explore the origins of their shame and guilt, challenge negative thought patterns, and develop coping strategies. Therapeutic work often includes exercises aimed at reshaping self-perceptions and building healthier emotional responses. Engaging in therapy not only provides tools for managing shame and guilt but also offers a supportive environment where individuals can process their feelings and gain insights into their emotional struggles.

Building supportive relationships is another key component in the recovery process. Strong, positive connections with friends, family, and support groups can provide the empathy, validation, and encouragement needed to counteract feelings of shame and guilt. Supportive relationships offer a sense of belonging and acceptance, which can be particularly healing for individuals grappling with deep-seated shame. Being part of a network where one feels valued and understood can help to counteract the isolating effects of these emotions. Moreover, sharing experiences with others who have faced similar challenges can provide additional perspectives and coping strategies, further aiding in the recovery process. Engaging in open, honest communication within these relationships can help individuals process their feelings and build a more balanced and positive self-view.

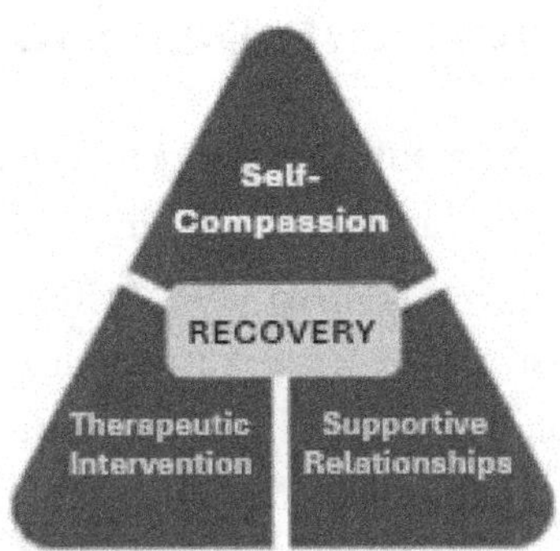
Self-
Compassion
RECOVERY
Therapeutic
Intervention
Supportive
Relationships

Self-compassion

Self-compassion is instrumental in the recovery from shame and guilt because it provides a fundamental shift in how individuals relate to themselves. Unlike self-criticism, which can deepen feelings of shame and guilt, self-compassion involves treating oneself with kindness and understanding, especially during times of difficulty or failure. This approach encourages individuals to recognize that everyone makes mistakes and experiences shortcomings, thus normalizing their struggles rather than personalizing them. By fostering a more forgiving and supportive internal dialogue, self-compassion helps individuals to counteract the harsh self-judgment that often accompanies shame and guilt, allowing them to approach their difficulties with greater emotional resilience and balance.

Incorporating self-compassion into one's recovery process can significantly alter the way individuals process and handle their emotions. When people practice self-compassion, they are more likely to engage in constructive self-reflection rather than punitive self-blame. This means that rather than spiraling into a cycle of excessive guilt or self-loathing, they can view their mistakes as opportunities for growth and learning. Self-compassion encourages individuals to adopt a perspective that acknowledges their human imperfections without letting these imperfections define their entire sense of self. This shift not only reduces the intensity of shame and guilt but also promotes a healthier, more realistic view of oneself and one's capabilities.

Furthermore, self-compassion facilitates emotional healing by creating a nurturing internal environment. This supportive self-relationship can buffer against the negative impacts of shame and guilt, enabling individuals to recover more effectively from these emotions. When people are kind to themselves, they are better equipped to engage in self-care practices and seek help when needed. This positive self-regard encourages proactive steps toward resolving underlying issues, whether through therapy, personal growth efforts, or constructive changes in behavior. Overall, self-compassion serves as a crucial foundation for rebuilding self-esteem and fostering a more positive, resilient outlook on life, thereby enhancing overall well-being and facilitating recovery from shame and guilt.

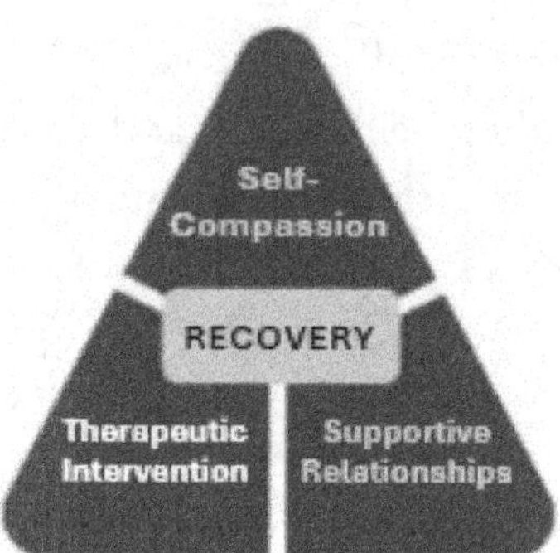
Self-
Compassion
RECOVERY
Therapeutic
Intervention
Supportive
Relationships

Therapeutic Intervention

Therapeutic intervention is crucial in the recovery from shame and guilt issues because it provides a structured and supportive environment for individuals to address and process these complex emotions. Trained therapists employ evidence-based techniques to help individuals explore the roots of their shame and guilt, which are often deeply ingrained and linked to past experiences or personal beliefs. Through therapeutic methods such as cognitive-behavioral therapy (CBT) or compassion-focused therapy, individuals can learn to identify and challenge distorted thought patterns that contribute to their feelings of unworthiness or remorse. This process is essential for breaking the cycle of self-blame and developing healthier ways of thinking about oneself and one's actions.

In therapy, individuals benefit from the guidance and support of a professional who can provide objective feedback and help them navigate their emotional struggles. The therapeutic relationship itself offers a safe space for individuals to confront and articulate their feelings without fear of judgment. This validation and understanding can be particularly healing for those who have experienced chronic shame or guilt, as it helps to counteract the isolation and self-criticism that often accompany these emotions. Additionally, therapists can introduce coping strategies and tools for managing distressing emotions, empowering individuals to handle their feelings more effectively and build resilience.

Therapeutic intervention also plays a critical role in fostering long-term recovery and personal growth. By working through shame and guilt with a professional, individuals can develop a deeper understanding of their emotional experiences and gain insight into how these feelings affect their behavior and relationships. Therapy can facilitate the development of self-compassion, improve self-esteem, and support the establishment of healthier interpersonal dynamics. Furthermore, ongoing therapy can provide a framework for setting and achieving personal goals, promoting continued self-improvement and emotional well-being. Overall, therapeutic intervention is a vital component in helping individuals heal from shame and guilt and achieve a more balanced and fulfilling life.

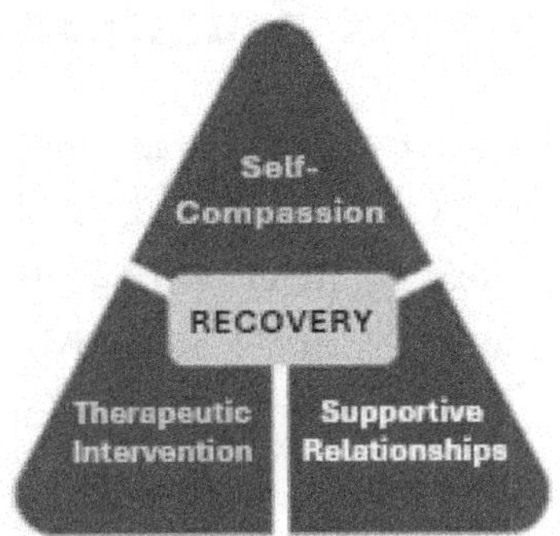
Self-Compassion
RECOVERY
Therapeutic Intervention
Supportive Relationships

Supportive Relationships

Supportive relationships are crucial in the recovery from shame and guilt issues because they offer validation, empathy, and a sense of belonging that can significantly alleviate the emotional burden of these complex feelings. When individuals are surrounded by caring and understanding friends, family members, or support groups, they are more likely to feel seen and valued despite their perceived flaws. These relationships provide a safe space for individuals to express their feelings without fear of judgment or rejection, which can help counteract the isolation and loneliness often experienced with deep-seated shame and guilt. The emotional support from others fosters a sense of acceptance and reassurance, which can be instrumental in reshaping one's self-perception and reducing the intensity of negative emotions.

In addition, supportive relationships can facilitate constructive dialogue and problem-solving, which is essential for addressing the root causes of shame and guilt. Loved ones can offer alternative perspectives and feedback that challenge distorted self-beliefs and encourage healthier ways of thinking about oneself and one's actions. This external validation can help individuals gain insights into their emotions and behaviors, promoting personal growth and emotional resilience. Moreover, the encouragement and accountability provided by supportive relationships can motivate individuals to engage in therapeutic practices, pursue self-improvement, and make positive changes in their lives, further aiding in their recovery process.

Finally, supportive relationships play a critical role in reinforcing self-compassion and self-care practices. When individuals are part of a network that emphasizes care and understanding, they are more likely to adopt similar attitudes towards themselves. Friends and family who demonstrate empathy and compassion can model healthy emotional responses and reinforce the importance of self-kindness and forgiveness. This positive reinforcement helps individuals internalize the principles of self-compassion and apply them to their own self-treatment. Ultimately, supportive relationships contribute to a more balanced and nurturing emotional environment, which is essential for healing from shame and guilt and achieving long-term well-being.

SUMMARY

Statistics on recovering from shame and guilt issues reveal that therapeutic interventions and supportive relationships significantly enhance recovery outcomes. Research indicates that therapy, particularly cognitive-behavioral therapy (CBT), is effective in treating emotional issues related to shame and guilt. A meta-analysis published in the "Journal of Consulting and Clinical Psychology" found that CBT reduces symptoms of shame and guilt in approximately 50-60% of patients, demonstrating its efficacy in addressing these complex emotions. Additionally, compassion-focused therapy, which targets self-criticism and promotes self-compassion, has shown positive results, with studies indicating a reduction in shame and guilt symptoms in about 60% of participants. These statistics highlight the effectiveness of structured therapeutic approaches in facilitating emotional recovery.

Supportive relationships also play a vital role in recovery, as evidenced by various studies. Research from the "Journal of Social and Personal Relationships" shows that individuals with strong social support networks experience quicker and more substantial improvements in mental health outcomes compared to those with limited support. For example, individuals who actively engage in support groups or maintain close connections with empathetic friends and family report a 40-50% increase in emotional well-being and a significant reduction in feelings of shame and guilt. These statistics underscore the importance of a supportive social environment in enhancing recovery and promoting overall emotional health.

However, the journey to recovery from shame and guilt is not uniform for everyone, and statistics also reveal challenges. A longitudinal study in "The American Journal of Psychiatry" found that about 30% of individuals struggling with severe shame and guilt may experience persistent issues despite therapeutic interventions. Factors such as the severity of underlying issues, the presence of co-occurring mental health conditions, and the quality of social support can impact recovery outcomes. This data emphasizes the need for personalized treatment approaches and ongoing support to address the complex nature of shame and guilt and improve long-term recovery prospects.

Invitation

Carrying **shame** and **guilt** can be metaphorically compared to lugging around a heavy backpack, which burdens every aspect of one's life. Just as a heavy backpack places constant physical strain on the shoulders and back, shame and guilt create a persistent emotional weight that drags down one's mental well-being. This weight can make daily tasks feel overwhelming and exhausting, as individuals struggle to manage the continuous pressure of self-reproach and remorse. Every step taken while burdened with shame and guilt can feel like a struggle, impeding one's ability to move forward with ease and clarity. The emotional load impacts not only personal happiness but also the ability to engage fully in life's activities and relationships.

The impact of this emotional weight is comparable to the physical discomfort of carrying an overly heavy backpack. Just as the weight can cause physical pain and restrict movement, persistent shame and guilt can lead to mental and emotional distress. Individuals may find themselves stuck in a cycle of negative self-talk and rumination, where their self-worth is constantly questioned and their actions scrutinized. This ongoing emotional strain can make it difficult to focus on positive aspects of life, hindering personal growth and well-being. In essence, the psychological strain of shame and guilt can constrain one's emotional freedom, similar to how a heavy backpack limits physical movement and comfort.

Releasing shame and guilt is akin to dropping a heavy backpack after a long hike. Just as letting go of a burdensome backpack provides immediate relief and a sense of liberation, letting go of shame and guilt can lead to significant emotional freedom and improved mental health. When individuals shed these heavy feelings, they often experience a newfound sense of lightness and clarity. This release allows them to move forward with greater ease, explore new opportunities, and engage more fully in their lives and relationships. Embracing practices such as self-compassion, therapy, and supportive relationships helps in metaphorically dropping the heavy backpack, enabling individuals to carry themselves more freely and healthily.

Shame can be triggered by various experiences and perceptions. Here are some typical sources of shame:

1. **Personal Failures**: Experiencing or perceiving oneself as failing in personal goals, responsibilities, or expectations, such as failing an exam, losing a job, or not meeting self-imposed standards.

2. **Social Rejection**: Feeling embarrassed or inadequate due to being excluded, rejected, or judged by others in social situations, such as not being invited to a social event or experiencing bullying.

3. **Behavioral Missteps**: Engaging in behaviors that go against one's own values or moral standards, such as lying, cheating, or acting in ways that one later regrets.

4. **Body Image Issues**: Negative feelings about one's physical appearance or body, including concerns about weight, shape, or other physical attributes, leading to a sense of inadequacy.

5. **Financial Struggles**: Experiencing financial difficulties or not meeting societal or personal expectations regarding financial success, such as struggling with debt or not achieving financial stability.

6. **Relationship Problems**: Issues in personal relationships, including conflicts, breakups, or difficulties in maintaining relationships, leading to feelings of inadequacy or unworthiness.

7. **Past Traumas**: Experiences of past traumas or abuse that lead to a sense of being fundamentally flawed or damaged, often exacerbated by societal stigmas or personal shame associated with the trauma.

8. **Cultural or Familial Expectations**: Failing to meet the expectations or norms set by one's culture or family, such as not fulfilling traditional roles or achieving certain milestones.

9. **Failure to Meet Social Norms**: Perceiving oneself as not

measuring up to societal standards or norms, such as expectations regarding career achievements, social status, or lifestyle.

10. **Mental Health Issues**: Struggling with mental health issues such as anxiety, depression, or addiction, and feeling shame about needing help or not coping effectively.

These sources of shame often involve a perceived violation of personal or societal standards, leading individuals to feel defective or inadequate. Addressing these feelings often requires self-compassion, support, and, in many cases, therapeutic intervention to overcome the impact of shame.

Guilt is often triggered by a range of behaviors and situations where individuals feel they have acted wrongly or failed to meet their own or others' expectations. Here are some typical sources of guilt:

1. **Hurting Others**: Causing emotional or physical harm to someone, whether intentionally or unintentionally, such as through arguments, betrayal, or neglect.

2. **Failing Responsibilities**: Not fulfilling responsibilities or obligations, such as missing a deadline, neglecting duties at work or home, or failing to meet promises.

3. **Dishonesty**: Engaging in deceitful behavior, such as lying, cheating, or stealing, leading to feelings of remorse and responsibility for the deceit.

4. **Neglecting Relationships**: Failing to provide support or attention to loved ones, such as not spending enough time with family or friends or neglecting a partner's needs.

5. **Making Mistakes**: Committing errors or poor decisions that lead to negative consequences for oneself or others, such as financial mistakes or poor judgment calls.

6. **Breaking Personal Values**: Acting in ways that conflict with one's own ethical or moral standards, such as behaving in a manner contrary to personal principles or beliefs.

7. **Not Living Up to Expectations**: Falling short of personal or societal expectations, such as not achieving goals or not performing at a desired level, leading to feelings of inadequacy.

8. **Being Unkind or Judgmental**: Acting in ways that are perceived as harsh, unkind, or judgmental towards others, leading to feelings of remorse over one's behavior.

9. **Neglecting Self-Care**: Failing to take care of oneself, such as neglecting health, personal well-being, or self-care practices, which can lead to feelings of guilt over not prioritizing self-care.

10. **Inaction in the Face of Need**: Failing to act or intervene when

one sees someone in need or distress, such as not helping someone in a crisis or ignoring an opportunity to assist others.

These situations often involve a sense of personal responsibility for the negative outcomes or failures, leading individuals to feel guilt and a desire to make amends or correct their actions. Addressing guilt often involves recognizing and learning from mistakes, making reparations when possible, and practicing self-forgiveness.

The Perils of Perfectionism

Perfectionism can pose significant perils, impacting both mental health and overall well-being. The relentless pursuit of perfection often leads to chronic stress and anxiety. Individuals who set excessively high standards for themselves may experience constant pressure to meet these ideals, leading to a cycle of never feeling good enough. This unrelenting quest for flawlessness can create an environment where minor mistakes are magnified, and failures are seen as catastrophic. Over time, this can result in burnout, where the stress of trying to maintain perfect performance leads to physical and emotional exhaustion, diminishing overall life satisfaction and functioning.

Another peril of perfectionism is its impact on self-esteem and self-worth. Perfectionists frequently tie their sense of value to their achievements and the ability to meet high standards. When they inevitably fall short of these unrealistic expectations, it can lead to feelings of deep inadequacy and self-criticism. This can foster a negative self-image where self-worth becomes conditional on perfection, rather than being inherent and stable. Such a mindset can erode confidence and make individuals more susceptible to depression and anxiety, as they continually feel they are failing to measure up.

Perfectionism also has detrimental effects on interpersonal relationships. The drive for perfection can lead to unrealistic expectations of others, often resulting in strained or conflict-ridden relationships. Perfectionists may demand the same high standards from those around them, leading to frustration and resentment. Additionally, perfectionists might struggle with vulnerability and authenticity, as they may hide their perceived flaws and failures from others to maintain an image of perfection. This can create barriers to genuine connection and intimacy, as relationships become more about maintaining a facade rather than fostering true understanding and closeness.

Perfectionism is a personality trait characterized by a relentless pursuit of flawlessness and excessively high standards for oneself. It involves a strong desire to achieve perfection and a tendency to evaluate one's worth based on the ability to meet these lofty expectations. Perfectionists often set unrealistic goals, are highly critical of their own performance, and may experience significant stress or dissatisfaction when they fall short of their standards. This trait can manifest in various areas of life, including work, academics, personal appearance, and relationships, leading to a preoccupation with error avoidance and an excessive focus on details. While striving for excellence can be motivating, perfectionism often involves an unhealthy obsession with being perfect, which can lead to negative emotional and psychological outcomes.

Downgrade Demands to a Preference

Downgrading demands to preferences involves shifting from rigid, perfectionistic standards to more flexible and realistic expectations. This process begins with acknowledging that perfection is an unrealistic and often unattainable goal. By recognizing that it's normal and acceptable to have preferences rather than demands, individuals can relieve some of the self-imposed pressure they place on themselves. This shift requires re-evaluating goals and standards to be more in line with what is practically achievable and personally fulfilling. For example, rather than setting an absolute expectation to excel in every aspect of life, individuals can set preferences that allow for fluctuations and imperfections, such as aiming to do one's best rather than being the best.

Adopting preferences instead of demands also involves adjusting one's mindset to embrace flexibility and self-compassion. Instead of viewing every shortfall or mistake as a failure, individuals can approach these situations with curiosity and acceptance. This means understanding that mistakes are part of the learning process, and that perfection is not a prerequisite for success or self-worth. By framing goals as preferences—such as wanting to improve a skill rather than demanding flawless performance—individuals can focus on progress rather than perfection. This mindset encourages a more balanced approach to personal and professional aspirations, where growth is valued over an unattainable ideal.

Implementing preferences in daily life requires practical adjustments to how one approaches tasks and relationships. For instance, setting realistic expectations for work projects or personal achievements can reduce stress and increase overall satisfaction. Instead of striving for perfect outcomes, individuals can prioritize effort and growth. In relationships, viewing preferences as guidelines rather than rigid rules can foster more supportive and understanding interactions. This approach allows individuals to adapt to changing circumstances and embrace a more flexible, compassionate attitude toward themselves and others. By making these adjustments, individuals can create a more fulfilling and less stressful life, where achievements are celebrated, and mistakes are seen as opportunities for learning rather than failures.

Here's an example of downgrading a demand to a preference:

"Boy, I am sure am eager to play golf today but if it rains us out, I can always reschedule. I'll do the next best thing and read a book on golf over a nice beverage inside a coffee shop."

In essence, if I get to play golf today that would be nice but if not, I'm going to enjoy today anyway. (an attitude of gratitude goes a long way for a healthy lifestyle).

Quotes on Shame/Guilt

"Shame is the most powerful, master emotion. It's the fear that we're not good enough."
— Brené Brown

"Guilt is perhaps the most painful thing to experience in life, but it's also a strong signal that we need to make amends and change our ways."
— Unknown

"Shame corrodes the very part of us that believes we are capable of change."
— Brené Brown

"Guilt is the gift that keeps on giving, while shame is the gift that keeps on taking."
— Unknown

"Shame is the intensely painful feeling or experience of believing we are flawed and therefore unworthy of love and belonging."
— Brené Brown

"We are all capable of shame and guilt, but it's how we manage and understand these feelings that truly defines us."
— Unknown

"Guilt is an emotion that tells us we have done something wrong, while shame is the feeling that we are wrong."
— Unknown

"Shame is like a cancer to the soul; it festers in secrecy and isolation, poisoning our self-worth."

— Unknown

"Guilt is the result of what we have done; shame is the feeling of who we are."
— Unknown

"To understand guilt is to acknowledge it, to understand shame is to accept that it does not define us."
— Unknown

When someone is struggling with a particular area or two, chances are they are "out of balance" with how life works. How does life work? Life works in threes.

If you're interested in personal topics like life, health, money or business topics like sales, time management and public speaking...Life Works in Threes! can shed some light on creating success in those areas.

The definition of TRIUNE is a group of three things; united. Being three in one, such as - humans are *mental, physical* and *spiritual beings.* The word TRYUNE is a play of the word TRIUNE, encouraging all to try this concept and help eliminate struggling unnecessarily.

LifeWorksInThrees.com

www.ingramcontent.com/pod-product-compliance
Lightning Source LLC
Chambersburg PA
CBHW061353140726
47997CB00003B/1194